WHERE SNOW LEOPARD PROWLS

WILD ANIMALS OF TIBET

WRITTEN AND ILLUSTRATED BY
NAOMI C. ROSE

For Snow Leopard and all the other precious beings of the animal kingdom. May you continue to bless us with your presence for a long, long time.

—N.C.R.

CONTENTS

*The love for all living creatures
is the most noble attribute of man.*

— Charles Darwin

WELCOME
TO THE
TIBETAN PLATEAU

The Tibetan *Plateau* is the largest and highest expanse of elevated land on Earth. It's about four times the size of Texas and reaches upwards to almost five miles high.

The world's tallest mountains, the Himalayas, tower over the plateau. Mt. Everest is their highest peak. It soars over 29,000 feet high. That's equal to a building with over 2,200 stories!

Many rare and wonderful animals make this special place their home.

TIBETAN PLATEAU FACTS

Location:	Central Asia
Average *altitude*:	Over 14,000 ft.
Size:	Over 960,000 square miles

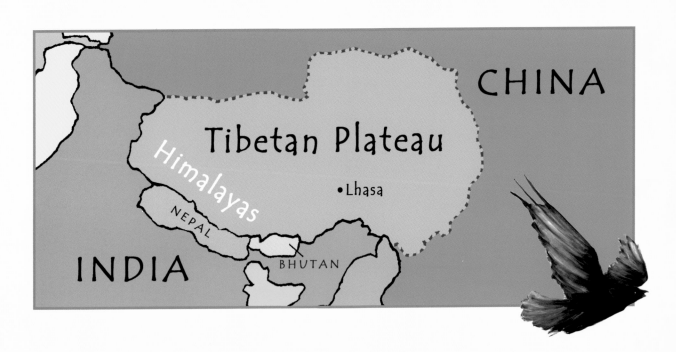

HABITATS

The Tibetan Plateau provides a wide range of *habitats*, including snow peaks, high deserts, rocky cliffs, grasslands, forests, rivers, lakes, and marshes.

Many of these habitats create unique environments for the animals.

Blue Sheep and Tahr on rocky cliffs

Snow Leopard on a snowy peak

Kiang in a grassland meadow

Red Panda in a forest

Black-Necked Crane in a marsh

SURVIVAL

Many animals in this book live in the higher regions of the Tibetan Plateau. Life there is not easy. Freezing temperatures, high altitudes, icy slopes, and less oxygen in the air create a harsh environment. Most animals in the world could not survive these challenging conditions.

Fortunately, the animals of the high plateau have adapted to these harsh conditions with special features. Ultra thick coats keep them toasty warm in the freezing cold. Large, rubbery hooves keep them steady on the slippery slopes. And extra *red blood cells* help them absorb more oxygen from the thin air.

Nature is a good mother, and sees well to the clothing of her many animals.

—John Muir

In the following pages, you'll meet some of these amazing animals.

DID YOU KNOW?

The higher regions of the Tibetan Plateau have freezing temperatures all year long. The average temperature is 25° F. This average dips to -40° F in winter.

Snow Leopard Facts

Body length: 4 to 5 ft.   Weight: 55 to 165 lbs.

Tail length: Up to 40 in.   Lifestyle: Solitary

SNOW LEOPARD

Snow Leopard leaps to a mountain ledge. Thick cushions of fur surround its paw pads protecting the paws from jagged rocks. The cushions also keep Snow Leopard from sinking in the snow.

It's wintertime and Snow Leopard's color has lightened. This helps Snow Leopard hide in the snow and sneak up on *prey* like Blue Sheep and Musk Deer. Strong back legs help Snow Leopard catch prey too. It can leap up to 50 feet. Snow Leopard is an excellent hunter and won't go hungry for long.

DID YOU KNOW?

To stay warm, Snow Leopard wraps its tail around its body and face, like a scarf.

SNOW LEOPARD CUBS

Snow Leopard's young live and hunt with their mother. When they are about eighteen months old, they leave to live and hunt alone.

The sky is cold and gray over the high plateau. Tibetan Wolf howls, and the wolves of its pack gather. The hunt begins. Tibetan Wolf travels with its pack in single file, stepping in the tracks of the wolf ahead. This creates an easier path in the snow.

Tibetan Wolf raises its snout, catching the scent of Wild Yak. Although Tibetan Wolf can run up to 40 miles an hour, Wild Yak gets away. The pack regroups and hunts again.

TIBETAN WOLF FACTS

Body Length:	Up to 4 ft.	Height:	Up to 3 ft.
Weight:	100 to 125 lbs.	Lifestyle:	Lives in packs

DID YOU KNOW?

Tibetan Wolf runs on its toes so it can travel faster and turn quicker.

WOLF PUPS

Tibetan Wolf's pups pounce on feathers, animal skins, and bones, then carry these "toys" around in their jaws. This helps train them to hunt when they are older.

TIBETAN WOLF

Wild Yak scrambles up an icy slope. Even though it's the largest animal of the plateau, Wild Yak doesn't slip or slide. Wide hooves keep it steady.

After the climb, Wild Yak digs under the snow with its horns. There it finds grass and twigs to eat. Wild Yak can also use its horns to fight off *predators* like Tibetan Wolf.

A blizzard of snow falls. Wild Yak's thick,shaggy coat protects it from the cold. Its short legs help reduce the loss of body heat. Wild Yak lies down, tucking its legs under its coat for extra warmth.

Wild Yak Facts

Height: Up to 6 ft.
Body length: Up to 11 ft.
Weight: Up to 2000 lbs.
Lifestyle: Lives in herds

Yak Cubs

Wild Yak's young stay near their mother until they're one year old. Then they remain in the herd to live with other yaks of all ages.

WILD YAK

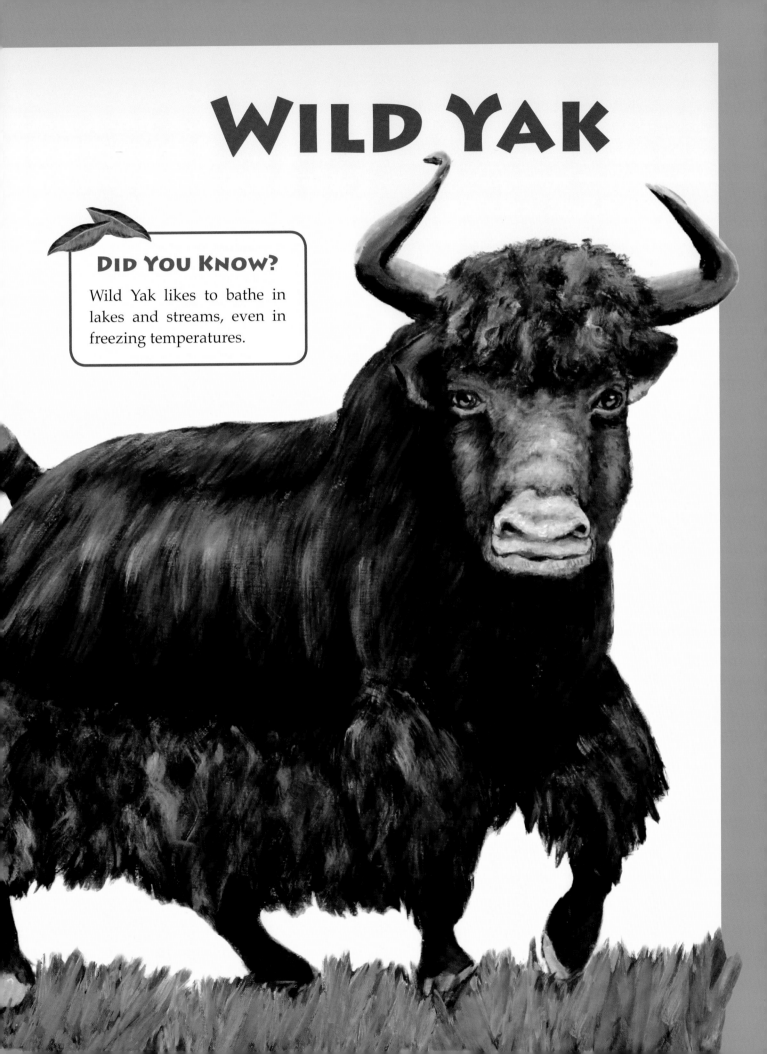

DID YOU KNOW?

Wild Yak likes to bathe in lakes and streams, even in freezing temperatures.

Tibetan Black Bear

Tibetan Black Bear wakes up in its cave. The long, cold winter is over. Black Bear didn't eat during *hibernation* and has lost a lot of weight. It's time to find food.

Black Bear lumbers into the sunlight and munches on berries and flowers. Then Black Bear heads to the river. Black Bear is a strong swimmer, and easily catches some fish to eat.

With a full stomach, Black Bear scurries up a tree and takes a nap. Now that the weather is warm, Black Bear will spend most of the day in trees, sleeping and avoiding predators like Tibetan Wolf.

Black Bear eats mostly at night. It has many foods to choose from: plants, insects, nuts, honey, fish, birds, and small animals. It has a lot of fattening up to do before next winter's hibernation.

Bear Cubs

Black Bear's cubs live with their mother for two to three years. When their mother senses danger, she grunts to tell the cubs to quickly climb high up a tree.

Black Bear Facts

Body length: 4 to 6 ft.   Weight: 110 to 440 lbs.   Lifestyle: Solitary

BLUE SHEEP

The spring sun warms the rocky terrain. Blue Sheep grazes on grass and other plants. Blue Sheep hears a twig break. Snow Leopard is near! Blue Sheep freezes. Its coat blends well with the cliffs. This gives Blue Sheep great *camouflage*, especially when it stands still. Snow Leopard leaps closer. Blue Sheep flees to a steeper ledge and stands still again.

BLUE SHEEP FACTS

Body length:	Up to 66 in.
Height:	Up to 32 in.
Weight:	120 to 180 lbs.
Lifestyle:	Lives in small flocks

DID YOU KNOW?

Rubbery hooves give Blue Sheep a good grip on the steep and slippery slopes.

KIANG

Kiang, a Tibetan wild donkey, bathes in a river. Others in its herd bathe too. Kiang does almost all its activities with its herd, including eating, drinking, and running.

In winter, Kiang's coat doubles in length. This helps Kiang stay warm. Kiang and its herd may also *migrate* to lower regions of the plateau to escape the cold. But winter is over for now, so Kiang and its herd dwell in the high grasslands.

After bathing, Kiang grazes on herbs and plants. Kiang catches sight of Tibetan Wolf creeping towards the herd. Kiang and its herd form a circle and kick their legs out. Finally Tibetan Wolf slinks away.

DID YOU KNOW?

Kiang's herd is led by an elder female.

KIANG FACTS

Shoulder height: 39 to 56 in.
Body length: 7 ft.
Weight: 550 to 880 lbs.
Lifestyle: Lives in herds

Chiru Facts

Body length: 33 to 39 in.
Weight: 57 to 88 lbs.
Lifestyle: Lives in small herds

Chiru Babies

Chiru's young can run just a few hours after they're born.

Did You Know?

Chiru runs in a zigzag course to help it escape from predators.

CHIRU

Chiru, a Tibetan antelope, grazes on grasses. The air is crisp on this late spring morning. Black Bear lumbers nearby, but Chiru is light and nimble and easily speeds away. Chiru has many air sacs in its nostrils. They help Chiru breathe in the thin air, allowing Chiru to run up to 50 miles per hour.

A strong wind blows over the mountain meadow. Chiru digs a shallow trench in the ground and climbs in. This protects Chiru from the wind. It also keeps Chiru out of sight of most predators. Chiru rests in the trench, waiting until twilight to graze again.

HIMALAYAN TAHR FACTS

Shoulder height:	2.1 to 3.3 ft.	Body length:	3 to 4.7 ft.
Weight:	79 to 189 lbs.	Lifestyle:	Lives in small herds

HIMALAYAN TAHR

Himalayan Tahr, a wild goat, lies hidden in the shrubs of a steep cliff. It has finished its morning grazing, and now wants to keep out of sight of predators.

In winter, Tahr's woolly coat and soft underfur keep it warm. Like Kiang, Tahr sometimes migrates to lower altitudes to escape the cold.

Winter is long past now. And the midsummer sun begins to set, turning the sky golden. Tahr ventures out from its hiding place to chomp on grasses and plants. Tahr suddenly stops chewing. Is that a predator it hears? Tahr doesn't want to wait to find out. Tahr's rubbery hooves help it grip the rocks as it flees.

DID YOU KNOW?

Himalayan Tahr's horns curve backward and may be up to 18 inches long.

TAHR KIDS

Tahr's young stay with their mother for almost two years. They learn to jump down steep cliffs by watching their mother jump first, then jumping to her as she waits.

MUSK DEER

Musk Deer rubs its scent on trees and rocks to mark its territory. This scent comes from the perfumed substance of Musk Deer's special glands. It also helps Musk Deer to be recognized by other deer. Suddenly, Musk Deer's ears quiver. A predator is near. Musk Deer is a swift runner, and leaps over 15 feet to get away.

In winter, food is scarce, and Musk Deer has to eat anything it can find, including twigs and bark. It's late summer now, and the meadow still has plenty of grasses and plants to eat. Musk Deer finds a safe place to munch.

DID YOU KNOW?

Unlike most male deer, Musk Deer doesn't have antlers. Instead, it has tusk-like incisors in its upper jaw.

MUSK DEER FACTS

Shoulder height:	20 to 21 in.
Body length:	2.8 to 3.3 ft.
Weight:	24 to 40 lbs.
Lifestyle:	Solitary

RED PANDA

Red Panda naps on a tree branch, covering its face with its tail. Its red fur is good camouflage against the red moss of the mountain forest.

Red Panda spends most of its time in trees, feeding on bamboo. It can eat up to 200,000 bamboo leaves a day.

Red Panda's nap is over. Time for a drink. Red Panda scurries down the tree and over to a stream. There, it plunges its paws into the water, then licks its wet paws.

Snow Leopard prowls nearby. Red Panda scampers up a rock column and out of danger. When Red Panda can't reach safety, it stands on its hind legs and strikes out with razor-sharp claws.

DID YOU KNOW?

Thick fur covers Red Panda's entire body, including the soles of its feet. This helps Red Panda stay warm in the cold winters.

RED PANDA FACTS

Body length: 20 to 25 in.
Weight: 7 to 13 lbs.
Lifestyle: Solitary

GOLDEN SNUB-NOSED MONKEY FACTS

Body length: Up to 25 in.
Tail length: 17 to 24 in.
Weight: Up to 77 lbs.
Lifestyle: Lives in large groups
               called troops

DID YOU KNOW?

Golden Snub-Nosed Monkey, along with other types of snub-nosed monkeys, lives at altitudes higher than any other monkey.

Golden Snub-Nosed Monkey

The autumn sun sprinkles through the trees. Sitting high on a branch, Golden Snub-Nosed Monkey combs through its fur with its fingers and teeth. Most of its time is spent in trees, eating, sleeping, and grooming. A predator begins to circle the tree below. Monkey speeds away on the upper *canopy*.

Very hungry after its flight, Monkey nibbles on leaves and other vegetation of the high mountain forest.

In winter, long thick fur, especially over Monkey's shoulders, keeps it warm. Monkey and its troop may migrate to lower altitudes to escape the cold.

Young Monkeys

Golden Snub-Nosed Monkey's young often chase and fight other young monkeys. This is good preparation for real battles when they grow older.

HIMALAYAN MARMOT

Himalayan Marmot perches on its hind legs and sniffs the air of the high meadow. With large beaver like teeth, it cuts and chews grasses and plants.

Marmot is a social animal. It communicates with other marmots through touch and sound. When a predator approaches, Marmot gives a high-pitched whistle to warn other marmots.

The last of the autumn leaves sail to the ground. Time for Marmot and the others to hibernate in their burrow underground. Once they are all inside, Marmot plugs the entrance with hay and earth. This helps to keep warmth in and predators out.

DID YOU KNOW?

Marmot's underground home includes resting areas and hibernation chambers. It even has a "bathroom."

HIMALAYAN MARMOT FACTS

Length: 2.6 ft.
Weight: 8 to 13 lbs.
Lifestyle: Lives in small groups called colonies

BLACK-NECKED CRANE

Black-Necked Crane sweeps its bill through the marshy water searching for food. It digs its bill into the mud for roots, insects, and small animals to eat. Crane straightens its neck to peer around. Snow Leopard! Crane dances wildly to distract Snow Leopard, then escapes to safety.

During migration, Black-Necked Crane feeds on stumps of grain left after harvest. It's time to migrate now. There's a chill to the air and winter is on its way.

BLACK-NECKED CRANE FACTS

Length: Up to 55 in.
Wingspan: Up to 7.8 ft.
Weight: 11 to 12 lbs.
Lifestyle: Lives in flocks.

DID YOU KNOW?

Black-Necked Crane dances often with other cranes.

LIVING IN HARMONY

The Tibetan people believe that nature is alive with spiritual beings. For example, each mountain is a god or goddess. Each lake is a lake spirit. Each tree is a tree spirit. These beings, together with humans and animals, form one family on Earth.

DID YOU KNOW?

The Tibetan name for Mt. Everest is Chomolangma. This name means Goddess Mother of the Snows.

Tibetans take great care to live in harmony with nature. And for a long time, their care helped protect and preserve the plateau's animals and habitats.

Now our modern developments and human activities challenge the survival of Snow Leopard and many other animals of the plateau.

Let's all do what we can to keep the animals and habitats healthy for years to come.

- Use Mother Nature's resources wisely.

- Use recycled products and recycle everything you can.

- Take public transportation, walk, and ride bicycles.

- Avoid using products that harm our environment.

- Leave wild plants and animals in their habitat.

- Don't buy products made from wild animals.

- Buy products that support wildlife and their habitats.

- Join wildlife organizations.

- And be sure to tell others about the amazing Tibetan wildlife!

THE ANIMALS THANK YOU!

ACTIVITIES

1. Name the animals on pages 26 and 27. *Hint: Each animal is described in this book.*

2. Write a story about wildlife on the Tibetan Plateau.

3. Draw or color a picture of one or more of the animals.

4. Write a poem about your favorite animal.

5. Become a pretend pen pal with an animal. Write the animal a letter about your life and ask about its life. Then write a letter from the animal, answering your questions.

Dear Snow Leopard,

6. Make a mask of one of the animals. Use paper plates, markers, and yarn to tie on the mask. Or use a mask kit found in craft stores.

DID YOU KNOW?

Tibetans create yak masks, then perform the yak dance. They believe this dance helps to bring harmony to our world and all of nature.

7. Perform a dance for your favorite animal. If you've made a mask, wear it in the dance.

8. Thank Mother Earth for taking care of the animals. Sing her a song. Or make a gift from natural objects, such as pebbles, leaves, and pine cones. Then leave your gift in a special spot in nature.

9. Visit nature centers and wildlife preserves. Keep a journal of the animals with descriptions, impressions, and sketches.

10. Find books and websites to learn more about Tibetan wildlife. Be sure to study the fish, lizards, snakes, frogs, and other critters that also live on the Tibetan Plateau.

For more activities, puzzles, and games, visit www.naomicrose.com/activities.

WORDS TO KNOW

Altitude: The height above sea level. Also known as elevation.

Camouflage: Coloring that blends in with the surroundings.

Canopy: Leafy upper branches of the trees in a forest.

Habitat: Natural environment of animals and plants.

Hibernation: Passing the winter in a sleep-like condition.

Migrate: To move seasonally from one region to another.

Plateau: Elevated expanse of land.

Predator: Animal that captures and eats other animals.

Prey: Animal hunted and eaten for food.

Red Blood Cells: Cells that supply oxygen to the body.

Honor all with whom we share the Earth:
Four-leggeds, two-leggeds, winged ones.

—Native American Elder

SOURCES

This book is a small sample of the many remarkable animals of the Tibetan Plateau. Here are some sources to learn more and get involved with these and other amazing animals.

Organizations

- American Himalayan Foundation: himalayan-foundation.org
- Izilwane: izilwane.org/about-youth.
- Saving Snow Leopards: snowleopardblog.com
- Seattle Woodland Park Zoo: zoo.org
- Snow Leopard Conservancy: snowleopardconservancy.org
- Snow Leopard Trust: snowleopard.org
- World Wildlife Foundation: wwf.org

Books

- *The Face of Tibet*, W. Chapman
- *Across the Tibetan Plateau*, R. Fleming Jr., D. Tsering, L. Wulin.
- *Himalayan Wildlife*, S. S. Negi

THANK YOU

Many thanks to those who offered their expertise in this book's creation: Nancy Craig, Santa Fe Educator; Pam Geernaert, Children's Librarian, Vista Grande Library; Nancy C. Hawkes, PhD, General Curator, Woodland Park Zoo, Seattle; Rick Janser and staff, Rio Grande Zoo, Albuquerque; Jennifer Madeiros and her 2007/2008 2nd grade class, Eldorado Elementary School; Margaret Nevinski, Children's Book Author; Brad Rutherford, Snow Leopard Trust; Neva Welton, longtime friend and supporter, and Robin Weeks, partner on the path.

Special thanks to those who helped make this book possible: Camille Cruse, Jean M. Day, Jean Ellermier, Matthias Fiechter, Tara Lumpkin, Michael K. McKinney, Sibylle Noras, Lucy O'Dea, Lanette Padula, Kathryn Pardo, Skyler Perkins, Losang Rabgey, Nancy Ruby, and Ella Roberts.

ABOUT THE AUTHOR AND ILLUSTRATOR

Rose with Luna, the Owl

Naomi C. Rose has been a lifelong lover of the natural world and a student of Tibetan culture and wisdom since 1994. She has won numerous awards and honors for her children's books, which include *Tashi and the Tibetan Flower Cure*, *Tibetan Tales for Little Buddhas*, and *Tibetan Tales from the Top of the World*. Her artwork has been exhibited throughout the United States.

Rose lives with her husband amidst the sacred red rocks of Sedona, Arizona. Please visit her website at naomicrose.com.

This book was created in partnership with:

Copyright © 2013 Naomi C. Rose

All rights reserved. No part of this book may be reproduced in any form or by any electronic or mechanical means, including information storage and retrieval systems, without permission in writing from the author or publisher.

 Dancing Dakini Press

DancingDakiniPress.com

Cover and Book Design by Naomi C. Rose
The text is set in Book Antiqua
The illustrations are rendered in acrylic on canvas

10 9 8 7 6 5 4 3 2 1
First Edition

Library of Congress Control Number: 2012939399

Hardcover ISBN: 978-0-9836333-0-3
Children/Wildlife/Tibetan

Snow Leopard painting on the cover and page 7 is based on a photo by Milan Trykar, courtesy of Snow Leopard Trust.

Printed in China.